Books by David Bottoms

POETRY

Vagrant Grace
Armored Hearts: Selected and New Poems
Under the Vulture-Tree
In a U-Haul North of Damascus
Shooting Rats at the Bibb County Dump
Jamming with the Band at the VFW (limited edition)

NOVELS

Easter Weekend
Any Cold Jordan

ANTHOLOGY

The Morrow Anthology of Younger American Poets (editor)

VAGRANT
GRACE

Vagrant Grace

POEMS

David Bottoms

COPPER CANYON
PRESS

The publication of this book was supported by grants from the Lannan
Foundation, the National Endowment for the Arts, and the Washington
State Arts Commission. Additional support was received from Elliott Bay
Book Company, Cynthia Hartwig, and the many members who joined the
Friends of Copper Canyon Press campaign. Copper Canyon Press is in resi-
dence with Centrum at Fort Worden State Park.

LIBRARY OF CONGRESS CATALOGING-IN-PUBLICATION DATA

Bottoms, David.
Vagrant grace: poems / by David Bottoms. – 1st ed.
 p. cm.
ISBN 1-55659-130-6 (alk. paper)
ISBN 1-55659-129-2 (pbk.: alk. paper)
1. Southern States Poetry. 1. Title.
PS3552.O819 V34 1999
811'.54 — DC21   99-6389
                                       CIP

9 8 7 6 5 4 3 2 FIRST PRINTING

COPPER CANYON PRESS
Post Office Box 271
Port Townsend, Washington 98368
www.ccpress.org

ACKNOWLEDGMENTS

Grateful acknowledgment is made to the editors of the following magazines, in which these poems first appeared: "Souvenir," "Fallout" in *DoubleTake;* "A Canoe" in *The Gettysburg Review;* "Night Company" in *International Quarterly;* "On Methodist Hill," "An Owl," "A Walk to Carter's Lake," "A Room on Washington Avenue," "My Uncle Sowing Beatitudes" in *The Kenyon Review;* "Living Lingerie: In the Modeling Parlor" in *The Paris Review;* "A Morning from the Gospel of John" in *Ploughshares;* "Bronchitis," "The Widower," "Our Presbyterian Christmas," "Their Father's Tattoo," "Country Store and Moment of Grace," "Steve Belew Plays the National Steel," "In the Wilderness," "A Sunday Dinner," "Occurrence in the Big Sky" in *Poetry;* "A Family Parade," "Flower in My Father's Parlor," "Night Strategies," "The Fisherman and the Little Fish," "My Daughter at the Gymnastics Party," "Heron Blues," "At the Grave of Martha Ellis" in *The Southern Review.*

Sincere thanks to Bob Hill, Dave Smith, and Ernest Suarez for their insightful readings of early drafts of these poems.

Grateful acknowledgment is made to Lonnie B. Holley for the use of his painting on the cover.

*This book is for
my mother and father,
and for Kelly and Rachel*

———————

All things aspire to weightlessness,
            some place beyond the lip of language,
Some silence, some zone of grace...

      – CHARLES WRIGHT

... I had taken the step into darkness. When that happens,
and then such a dream comes, one feels it as an act of grace.

      – CARL JUNG

My heart was cloven and there appeared a flower,
and grace sprang up...

      – *The Odes of Solomon*
      TRANSLATED BY HARRIS AND MINGANA

Contents

VAGRANT
GRACE

PART I

Bronchitis

I

Rough sleep from the room across the hall.
Mouth open, my daughter breathes the little noise of wheels
on dry axles. I've cut the ceiling fan
to hear her, but rain intrudes against the house,
along with something quieter
and more disquieting,
some muffled trudge
like soldiers crossing our soggy yard,
ghosting cannons east again toward Kennesaw.

I mark my page with a postcard
and delay General Sherman on his blaze to the sea.
Shadow faces on the curtains grimace
and sneer, a burlesque of hysteria,
but nothing as cadaverous
as history. The truth is,
my eyes tend to tire and blur.

Cough and ragged wheeze, and outside
in the driveway
the wind rakes the lid of a garbage can.
All the loose uncertainties of fatherhood grate
in the joints of my chair.

2

A bloated rail yard, hardly more,
yet miserably strategic...
Off to the north cannons booming on Kennesaw, sullen
and dull, like heavy luggage tossed from a train.
Shouting in the houses, haste of foot traffic
and nervous horses, wheels
and mules stirring the streets into dust,
everything flying into wagons, the roads clogging,
the sky clogging.

Then after days, an odd silence –
the Federals flanking east of the mountain, crossing
the Chattahoochee. Skirmishes dying into siege.
The first shell whistling into the city
kills a three-year-old girl
playing with her dog in the street.

Under the traffic light
at Ellis and Ivy,
I've tried to gauge some vague geography lifted
from books. That was the crossroads,
but which was the corner the house sat on?
Two parking decks, Wachovia Bank,
a hot dog vendor,
a sidewalk gallery of African art –

3

I think of her sporadically, shell crater and spaniel,
powder stench, geyser of dust settling
as her mother staggers
onto the porch –
and I wonder whose story this is. I don't know,
only imagine the color of her eyes or hair,
or what she might have weighed
on the feed-store scales,
or what piece of ground they laid her in.
I don't even know the name on the stone
they must've placed at her head.

Neither, it seems,
does the man who wrote the history,
who mentions her only as a footnote in the abstract
strategies of war.
Whose story then? Whose history shadowed
or foreshadowed, if not mine?
Or yours?

The book lies open on my lap.
The postcard is from a friend in Washington –
cherry blossoms on the White House lawn.
A blizzard, he writes,
*is pounding the city, the homeless
have invaded the monuments and galleries.*

On Methodist Hill

for Joy Mallard

I

Shab of a plundered tomb, crust and leaf-stain,
litter of wet newspaper, sandwich wrapper, pizza box, stench
of sardine and wine –
in the wind it hisses slightly,
or sighs like a choir before the first note sung,
then nothing much as I walk my daughter up the marble steps.

Shadows jump-start the spirit – already an echo
this lingering absence
can't quite snuff. We pause
on the great portico before the blinded windows,
the chained-up door.
Echo of what?

Those feet that grooved these steps –
how to raise them
like numbers off old calendars,
how to follow down the cracked sidewalks of Church Street
and Main, Jarvis, Juniper,
into those bright houses renovated for offices,
or others boarded and gray, slumping
into weedy yards, when
my daughter keeps pulling me toward graves?

2

Where are the images that edified?
The olive trees
blue in the torches of the crowd, the tumble of clouds
hovering, the disciple raising his blade of light –
where have they fled
with that falling ear? And the night shadows
the lambs threw onto the gravestones,
the twelve at table,
the Christ in his purple agony of glass?

I pry slack board and rub a window –
stacks of hymnals, stems of charred roses
sagging in a corner – then a siren whirls us around.

An ambulance threading traffic on Main
swerves up the hill where the Canton First Baptist
raises its stable and star.
A feeling brushes close
like a scarf,
then boots a few leaves down the steps.

3

It is night,
and from the fires burning in the distance
we imagine cold, windy even among the olive trees.
Those who have come with him, three of the true
and warned to be watchful,

have fallen away with their light
to sleep off the paschal wine, four cups by law.

Something is stirring, he knows.
To the meal he had not invited his women,
or his family. Surely some violence
is closing a fist, and farther off in the trees,
he falls down and prays. In the breathing
of his friends he hears his loneliness.
He asks that the cup might pass,
his hands are covered with bloody sweat.
For an hour he prays,
but already he's foreseen – the rubble
of the temple, the three denials,
the trial and scourge, the veiled
and dusty road to Emmaus,
and maybe even as far as this church
hollowed and crumbling on a hill of weeds
where a four-year-old climbs a vandalized angel
as her father begins, unaccountably, to weep.

A Family Parade

I

Sparks off the sequins of majorettes,
off sun-flaked tiaras
and the blurred propellers
of fire batons dragging that off-key glare of French horn
and tuba, cornet, trumpet, trombone.
I edge through the stench
of crowd-sweat and popcorn to glimpse the mayor
in his dealership Lincoln, and the clowns
on stilts, the flowered truck beds
of Lions and Kiwanis,
the Model-T Ford with two front ends, whirling and braking
and whirling again, wild hair
of the drivers slinging flames through the windows,
and the tiny fire truck waving its rubber ladder,
the bucket brigade dousing the crowd
with confetti...

Somewhere up Main Street
I hear them idling, the motorcycle corps
of The Ancient Arabic Order
of the Nobles of the Mystic Shrine, far around the curve
past the antebellum library waiting
to be reborn in brick and glass, their engine noise
deadened by polka and crowd, but revving

as I close my eyes harder
to catch them threading the sawhorses
of the Canton Police, their flashing red signals
not quite muted
in sunlight glancing off chrome...

Look out, lady, I'm coming through...

2

Fat sun like a headlight
and a shower of petals, dogwood and pear,
a few confused raindrops speckling the asphalt...
Rachel banks on a training wheel, veers
toward her mother, then cuts away,
                                        flag of the fifty states
ruffling from her basket, a bouquet of balloons
off her fender...

A rolling quack
and rattle, bulb horn, mouth harp, tambourine,
Sousa-blasting boom box bungeed
to my carrier,
                    I circle them down the streets of the suburb,
clowning for a block with my feet on the handlebars,
tipping my sombrero at kids
dodging sprinklers, barbecue jockeys saluting
with their spatulas.

3

Finally, yes, I know this is about eternity,
this circling, this following,
and, of course, that irredeemable taunt of memory,
without which we'd have no ghosts to lead us...
the way my father leads his pack into the Snake Slither,
the Rolling Circle, the Figure 8.
Out of the way, lady...
and I nudge past the big hip draped with shopping bags
to hang my elbows
over the prickly ropes.

Siren and foghorn, and the gutted racket of tailpipes
as he rears onto one wheel, glasses in flames
and green trousers ballooning,
tassel of spun gold trailing from his fez...
Yes, here he comes again, noble

and father, clutching
and revving, making his circle,
headlight of his motorcycle searing my brain,
the eyes in his lenses catching my wave,
or not, as he weaves back
into his turn...

I turn also
and lift my glasses to catch Rachel's eyes...

sunlight through maple leaves strobing the pavement,
and that unmuffled grace
of costume and pomp
fading in the glare of a drugstore window.

PART II

The Widower

Already he saw it all,
rocked back against his tobacco counter, staring out
the barred window of his grocery
at the highway and the green wilderness of kudzu
quilting the hills beyond.
Often a customer standing inside the door
had to shuffle or cough, or a stranger in a hurry
might slap the top of the Coke box.
I raided the ice-cream cooler a hundred times.

On hot days a fan turned its slow head
in a corner, and in winter
the fat stove sighed over the oiled floor.
A gospel quartet sang on the radio,
promises that may have signified.
For a clean high tenor
his head would tilt,
and he rarely moved unless he had to.

The spirit had simply settled into a chair
to rock for twenty years.
It was as though he'd found a window into himself,
or out, and only occasionally,
when the store was empty, would he turn
to check the register or the meat freezer,
the aisle behind the dress patterns

and the racks of thread,
the way a traveler broken down in the country
will look up the road
for help he knows isn't coming,
or a man who's lost a good watch
will continue to glance
at his wrist.

Souvenir

Heavier than a brick, but finely wrought and shiny,
this bronze horse with a clock in its belly
my father bought at a show in Knoxville.
Through most of my childhood
it poised on a doily on the living-room table,
front leg crooked, mane and tail ruffled
in a make-believe wind.
Mother beside him in the cab,
he traveled to horse shows then, pulling
a trailer, while I stayed behind
with grandparents, pouting,
though lavishly bribed with toys and boots,
and once a genuine Gene Autry saddle.
He wanted me to love horses,
and I did, without fear,
even the Shetland that pitched me like a greenhorn
into the grassy pasture, and the colt
that flayed my leg from ankle
to knee on a splintered rail of the riding-ring fence,
but never this thing gone gaudy and blotched,
hooves cracked, a crafty tick
always in its belly
like some curiosity dragged into a city
to amaze and lull, biding the moment
of surprise –
which is all I have of his horses,

except for one photo. Ten years
past his war wounds here, he's almost healed –
a young man in a Panama and tailored brown suit,
riding a high-stepping Tennessee walker.
The horse's name is Happy Sunrise.

Fallout

First a noise under the kitchen,
then a week later
that same chug and scrape under my bedroom floor.
Out my window I watched them roll those wheelbarrows
across our backyard, down to the dam of our neighbor's pond.
At dinner my father's face was drawn,
for days on end my mother burned the rolls.
Who knew exactly what was going on,
though fear was everywhere like odor
from a mildewed carpet?
In geography class someone charted a map.
Boats from a foreign country were sailing toward Cuba,
an island of cigars. The boats were from Russia,
a land of red bears, and they carried in their hulls
bombs of hot dust.

Then the thing was finished.
We bought a model train and planned a game room –
Ping-Pong and bumper pool, Monopoly and the game of Life.
But that was a dream no one wanted to enter.
It was a steep flight and damp,
and once in midsummer after rain had sogged the yard,
I saw a copperhead drag its tail over the stoop.
There were spiders, too, and other dreads,
not the least of which were the fears themselves
we'd taken from the house

and shelved down there with the dried and canned goods,
all those basics reserved for the future,
pressed into a dark we hoped, in our reprieve,
would become more and more remote.

Flower in My Father's Parlor

Like the magnolia blossom in the vase on his counter,
waxy as the moon, flowering near the color
of twilight, the mysteries had opened a few buds
that year, spread moist petals,
fascinated for a moment...
He tied the straps on his plastic gown, pulled
a glove halfway to his elbows,
and seemed embarrassed by the glare in the room –
the stainless tub, the stool and table –
or else by something in my face.

Small noise of traffic, but the radio helped,
a mandolin, a guitar, so that whatever
I'd burst into the room for
lost its urgency.
From the front porch I must have watched an hour
as a star muscled light through the streetlamps,
and the gold moon blackened the cherry,
a trick of leaves and shadow.

I could've crouched behind those boxwoods,
could've found that slit where the shade
didn't quite meet the sill.
But who really wants those petals to open?
Still, in the bad sleep of middle age, they open –
the pink sponge like an orchid

in his hand, and the sheet
on that stainless table
a white flower
all children wither into.

An Owl

Twice through my bedroom window
I've seen the horned owl drop from the oaks to panic
the rabbit in my neighbor's backyard.
Last night he paced for an hour across the top
of the cage, scrutinizing
the can of water, the mound of pellets,
turning his genius to the riddle
of the wire, while under him
the rabbit balled like a fat carnation in the wind.

Both of the terriers yapped from their porch
but the owl never flinched, pacing,
clawing the wire, spreading wings like a gray cape,
leaping, straining to lift the whole cage,
and the cage rocking
on its stilts, settling, and rocking again,
until he settled with it, paused,
and returned to a thought.

And the rabbit, ignorant of mercy,
curled on itself in that white drift
of feathers?

Wait, three years and I haven't escaped the child
I saw at Northside the night
my daughter was born,

a little brown sack of twigs
curled under glass, eyes bulging,
trembling in the monitors,
and the nurses
rolling the newborns out to nurse,
and the shadows sweeping the nursery.

Night Strategies

I kept brushing the cloth over the pouch of her stomach,
the cherubic and slightly chafed
folds of her hips,
remembering the voice rising off my radio,
a girl in Sarajevo, sixteen,
quivering between a translator and the thuds
of local shelling.

Just after dark she'd heard shouts in the street,
trash cans knocked over, panic
and the rumble of trucks,
and was crossing the room to blow out a lamp
when a soldier kicked in the door.

That dry wind in her throat,
what did it whisper about the authority of grief?

And when he pulled out of her,
when he buckled and holstered his pistol,
he went to the window and called in two comrades.
They left her naked on a bloody cot.
She wept, she said, but not inconsolably
like her mother, who clawed all night at the tiles
of their mosque.

I lathered the cloth with our wafer of soap
and dabbed at my daughter's stomach and thighs,

knowing the only answer I have
is this nervous
exaggeration of tenderness,
and that every ministry of my hand, clumsy
and apologetic, asks her
to practice such a radical faith.

The Fisherman and the Little Fish

for Rachel

Calm water
and the boat pushing out across a gray skin of shadow...
Cast after cast, he reeled the gold spoon through the cove,
then the red spinner with the rooster tail,
the flat-headed jelly worms
that sparked underwater like mica,
and nothing to show for his rising in the dark,
his dressing on the porch so as not to awaken them.
Now it was late, the sun above the mountains,
already warming the gunwales.
Soon they'd be up and ready for hiking.

Across the lake a fish eagle watched from a dead spruce,
a crow clocked time across the Flathead valley.
Then the strike.
                    It ran, turned
and ran again. But rose too easily into his hand.

He looked at the fish, the smooth grain of skin
turning colors in his palm,
the sun-glossed eyes, the pinched mouth gasping
as though to say, *Too small, throw me back,
next year I'll make a better meal.*

He thought of her waking in the rented cabin, sitting down
with her mother to milk and cold cereal.

He eased the fish into his cooler.
Hardly pan-size, true, but she'd never tasted trout...
and this one was a rainbow,
what she'd wished for
yesterday as they waited out the downpour.

Our Presbyterian Christmas

Wings and halos,
all she'd talked about for weeks, and there they hung,
two racks sparkling like silver dust.
A woman holding a clipboard licked
the tip of a pencil. What was my daughter's name and age?
The fours would be shepherds, the fives
would be angels.
                We were late and huffing
and thought we'd misheard.
Rachel looked at me, eyes wrinkled,
and turned to the table
where a pile of rags lay like dead leaves,
then faced in tears that stony Presbyterian stare.
She could be an angel next year,
the woman said, if they let the children choose,
they'd all be angels.

Glare of headlights and sooty streetlights, drizzle
and a sharp wind from the north.
But we wanted to walk, so I buttoned her coat,
dabbed with a cuff at her eyes.
A block up Church Street
she stepped ahead –
the roofs along the square were struggling to catch fire,
and the bandstand in the park, the magnolias budding
red and gold, their flickering branches
sagging with stars.

My Daughter at the Gymnastics Party

When I sat for a moment in the bleachers
of the lower-school gym
to watch, one by one, the girls of my daughter's kindergarten
climb the fat rope hung over the Styrofoam pit,
I remembered my sweet exasperated mother
and those shifting faces of injury
that followed me like an odor to ball games and practices,
playgrounds of monkey bars
and trampolines, those wilted children sprouting daily
in that garden of trauma behind her eyes.

Then Rachel's turn,
the smallest child in class, and up she went, legs twined
on the rope, ponytail swinging, fifteen, twenty,
twenty-five feet, the pink tendrils of her leotard
climbing without effort
until she'd cleared the lower rafters.
She looked down, then up, hanging in that balance
of pride and fear,
                    then glancing
toward the bleachers to see if I watched, let go
her left hand, unworried by that boy
with the waffled skull, stiff and turning blue
under the belly of a horse,
or the Christmas Eve skater on Cagle's Lake,
her face a black plum
against the bottom of the ice.

Their Father's Tattoo

Eagle lifting a rose? Or was it a heart?
And each remembering differently through her own wounds
and having to know and remember correctly,
sees nothing to do
but enter on the sly the little parlor
where their father lies on the velvet bier, or the body
of their father, as they say,
dressed in his best Western shirt and bandanna, new Levi's
pulled down over lizard-skin boots.

Beyond the curtain a steady chatter circles the porch,
and against those utterances of grief
and consolation, an electric guitar
barks down Grange Street, something like coyotes
in the hills above the sheepfold.

The arm they're after is wedged against the wall
and they struggle to slide back the bier...
an inch or two, a little more
then the thumb drops off his buckle
and the arm falls.
                Voices of family
flutter in the hallway, a shadow brushes the curtain.
They lift the arm, a log in a sleeve,
and lay it across his chest.
One tugs lightly at the shoulder of his shirt,
and, cut down the back,

it peels away, the other raises the camera.
Years of envy and misgiving,
malice of injury and middle age,
still they smile at that flash of old mischief.

PART III

Country Store and Moment of Grace

for Richard Bausch, Joe Hendricks
& Tom Trimble

Oxford heels
hooked on the bottom rung, he rocks his straight chair
against his counter. Flick of his yo-yo
and he's walking the dog – wanting no trouble, pondering
in his afternoon daze the promised serenities
of the afterlife.
                    Pot-gut stove and wood sizzle,
and the raw smell of bologna and cheese, rack
of Slim Jim and jerky, Tom's Snacks,
peppermint, drift of kerosene from a paint can,
and from where he sits,
                              glassed sweetness
of stacked tobacco, Chesterfield and King Edward,
Beechnut, Red Man, Bull of the Woods.

Cold in this memory,
                          and through the barred window
the low sky flaunts the rags of winter.
A gospel quartet weaves harmonies
through the radio...
and the darkness seeping up from the freshly oiled floor
won't be beaten by three naked bulbs
choking on greasy cords.

Yes, ánd those wallowing clouds
of discontent...
barbershop, pool hall, beauty-parlor rumor
of discontent rising from the Ralph Bunche School...

Where? That shamble of brick off the Waleska Road
we pass on the way to my uncle's farm...
and one afternoon
when the store's jammed up around the stove,
I zip my jacket to pump a tank of gas –
rusted-out pickup, sagging
on its springs,
                    and looped around the rearview
a stiff noose
hanging like a pair of dice.

All through my childhood
I hardly heard a story unfold around that stove...
a curse spit onto its belly,
or a wisecrack following some trail of gossip,
but mostly grunts
                    or nothing at all
as my grandfather bagged the scribbled-out groceries.

38

Where were the storytellers I'd grow up
to hear about?
        Brooding or tongue-tied,
worn-out in their walked-down boots and overalls shabby
with clay and tobacco juice,
or crippled, or sick,
            coming straight
from the mill where they'd retched out their lungs
into smoking-booth peach cans,
               weak
and lint-crowned, wanting to get home.

In middle age,
in those first leaf-turns before the smudging into winter
when the bird feeders are abandoned
to squirrels and frost
and everything alive is sacking it up
               or packing
it in for the season,
the memory becomes portentous,
            like some newfound gospel
promising, finally, the whole fantastic story
and unscrolling into fragments.

———————

Brass glow of charcoal
and stench of beefsteak rising into the low clouds,

all over the suburb burnt offerings going up
under the drizzle of leaves...

Rachel rakes a few into a pile the wind disperses,
and again I'm drawing parallels
to the memory...
                    gusts behind the eyelids,
mulch of the cosmic swirl...

Eleven or twelve, I bop into the store...

blue smoke around the woodstove
                              where a few men lean
against the ice-cream box – the man with a hook
who left his hand in Italy,
the logger who walks on the side of his foot,
another I don't know
scraping his thumbnail with the blade of a barlow –
jeans and jackets, a cap with earflaps,
scrub beards icing into sideburns.

I squeeze past the bread counter
and jerk a few balloons from a glass jar, water bombs
for the Boy Scouts.

Nigger knocking? the clubfoot grins,
                              shaking peanuts
into his Coke bottle.

My grandfather, saying nothing, rings the cash register,
and the blue Prince Albert drifts
across the store.
                 Blood rush and the white haze
of laughter...

Whose laughter? And who am I here
pushing through the screen and into the air?

———

Blam! and shoulder-kick
and the barbed stink of gunpowder blowing across the field,
one or two targets
                 rattle on their wires
and behind them a trembling of needles and leaves
dangling over that outfield fence...

Turkey shoot sponsored by the Canton Little League,
and me running targets
across a pasture
                 my father has turned into a diamond...

Smudge pots glowing
through rust, folding table of shotguns, cherished
blued steel cradled in the plush
of unzipped cases,
and a lost face at the judge's table
                              shuffles a stack
of riddled targets, gauging in a huddle of men
the two pellet holes
closest to the center of the cross.

Compass legs rise off a target,
my grandfather's pellet
                    a chicken whisker off.

———————

Those little self-judgments, needle jabs of regret...
easy enough to stomach
with a shake of the head, a sour grin,
then the grim walk home, alone,
                              pockets empty, sky empty...

and late into the night
those prickly fingers of moonlight
pointing from the bedroom wall, those sweaty sheets,
that black noose of fuchsia
                    dangling from the planter.

Whenever I think I know about grief,
I imagine an only son lost
in the Pacific,
                an ear to the Philco for sketchy news...
Coral Sea, Midway, Guadalcanal...
and picture my grandmother collapsing one morning
by the mailbox,
crushed letter like a rock in her hand.

Fifteen months she thought him dead
                              and fell every evening
at the altar of Oakdale
until a woman in the church dreamed him wounded
but faceup,
                alive in burning water...

Tears and worn-out prayer bones
and everything else is gravy –
                        King James Bible,
ragged paperback *Gone With the Wind,*
green stamps, soda caps,
a few mail orders collecting around Christmas...
pans of Dr. Pepper
                        heating on the stove...
rags for quilts, a box of buttons,
thimbles and needles,

and unraveling off-key in the kitchen
the scratchy thread of one old song,

when the shadows

of this life have grown...

———

Yes, late into the night while the gray needles
slap the window
and again at sunrise, and again on the last waves of light
sifting through these shedding maples...

like the spring catalog of Montgomery Ward, waterlogged
and fat as a Masonic Bible,

sprawling three days
in their drive, drying its leaves in the sun.

I've robbed it from the mailbox
straight to the yard swing
to savor it most of the afternoon –

the spinners and lures,
those willowy rods that thrashed the riffles
of northern rivers...

So when I leave it open
in the swing to soak up an hour of evening rain,
I'm not stunned
to find it like something hurt

                    wrapped in towels
on the kitchen porch,
nor stunned now to glimpse again her face
that only time I saw her weep.

———

Sputter of choked engine, cough
and snarl,
          and a spume of dusty smoke wallows the back fence.
Our neighbor, the broker, revving his leaf blower...
like a bird from prison bars has flown,
and the oily cloud sifts through the trees...
so be it. Yes, so be it. Amen to the tidy suburban driveway,
to all souls sweeping up loose scraps.

Jesus of Oakdale,
            of Philadelphia and Macedonia,
Savior of the lost souls of Shiloh,
who stills the heart's waters at the altar of Soul Harbor,
raise your staff out of those stained windows
and shepherd these sheep
               across the hills of remorse.

———

A hundred yards south of my grandfather's grocery –
ours is the scrawny house of green shingles, rusted screens
on the side porch,
rock arch around the door.

Television in the living room, Arthur Godfrey
or Ed Sullivan, and a juggler spins plates on tall sticks
as my father and I watch from the couch...
Sweet smell of corn
and barbecued chicken,
                              which means it's Sunday...

Horns blare from the highway, south from the Trading Post,
loud and louder,
then right outside our door
                              a legion of noise.
I jump toward the window
and get jerked back,
                              my father's fist on my belt, holding,
his head shaking, a look on his face.

My mother walks in from the kitchen, dishrag wringing
a water glass. Her eyebrows wrinkle...

three or four minutes before the Empire passes.

———

Lipscomb, Lusk, Dilworth, Pope,
the names wash in
like familiar smells – pine straw, dog lot, cow manure,
leather tack and the wet hides of horses –
tough as their ax handles, blunt
as the pistol butts hanging from their pockets,
though not the tall man in his eternal bibs
frayed at every corner and crease,
who on Saturdays leaned over the ice-cream box
like a mourner
                              over a casket,
and brought out for the small girl in coat-rags
near the grill of the stove
                              one frostbitten hunky.

Depression-era photo, sharp bone, tow hair,
sagging eyes...
                              and though she hears nothing,
and speaks it back like a Holiness tongue,
all rough talk has ceased,
                              the air
she moves through like an aisle of grace.

The man with one arm
                              puts a Hershey's in her palm,
another fills her pocket with peanuts.
Smoke and shadows...
                              but nothing
in those shadows as luminous as her face.

Close it down, Dilworth says...

Swish of a blade on a slick whetstone, and out the window
a yellow frenzy of snow...

Close it down, he says,
                              fore I let Lyndon Johnson run it.

Dilworth, the roughest and loudest,
though none are boasters or idle talkers.

So nods Lipscomb, so nods Lusk.

And what more frightening
                              than a room of quiet men?

A Christmas story often told.
Canton, Georgia: black section, Stumptown,
and who has seen snow only twice in her life,
and that so long ago
                              she recalls it as sugar, flour, salt,
sits in her kitchen all morning
and through the clear windowpane
watches a sky staining gray
                              over a bristled ridge of pine.

He's late today,
            which means the woods behind the school
will be one pine less thick,
which means the Singer will need to be rolled
into the bedroom, the rocker drawn
to the side
            of the fireplace,
which means the balls of cloth and glass
can come out of their boxes
                        in the hall closet...
mistletoe and pine boughs,
candles lined on the windowsills...

And as the sky over the ridge thickens like night,
she thinks of stars,
                cinnamon stars
sprinkled over icy borders of cake, stars of red tinsel
hanging from the mantel,
                    the heavy brass star shining
like gold behind the white candle,
the evening star rising behind those clouds
like a bright eye
burning, unseen, all night.

Then who has seen snow only twice in her life,
who thinks she loves
                every kind of star, sees climbing
the road beside her house
the dull yellow star on the door of a Chevy
and feels down her nerves

                              the ice
of her whole head frosting white, a shiver
against terrible weather.

                    ———————————

True story. Small-town courthouse, movie-set live oaks
sagging over a scruffy lawn, cigar butts
and acorn-fall,
                    marble steps up to the marble portico,
and climbing them one out-of-town lawyer,
young and wiry, dapper in suit, bow tie, suspenders,
not yet a headliner,
                              not yet the winner of big cases.
A civil suit
in the county seat of corruption...
already he knows the defendant's attorney
is the judge's brother. Still, the truth and the law.

First question from the judge,
"Mr. Cook, have you and your client made an honest attempt
to settle this case?"
                    Bobbie Lee stands up
and strokes his goatee,
"Why, yes sir, we made an offer of twenty thousand."
"Oh, no, Mr. Cook," the judge
shakes his head, "we couldn't possibly pay that..."

Dead are the corrupt
and no less dead are the less corrupt...
and this evening a crystal dusting of sunlight layers
the backyard with shadow and near-shadow.

Red poplar leaf and oak leaf,
                            and a few scruffy sparrows
still foraging the feeders...
no swaggering robins,
                            no wild canaries
with their little yellow crowns... *Like a bird
from prison bars,* yes. The hummingbird feeder droops
from its branch
like a Japanese lantern.

December 1960. Weekend of rumor
and black weather blowing in from Alabama, two cars
        burned
on the curb in front of the Canton Theater...
Then that familiar crunch
of gravel as a car rolls up to his gasoline pumps.
Brooding men and veil of blue smoke
and the hot belly of the stove...

                              The car door shuts
but no one glances up.
Creak of the screen and the big door opening...

Dilworth pushes off the drink box, closes his knife,
Pope takes out his stogie and spits
on the stove.
                    Sizzle
and a shifting of logs, and the high wheeze
of wood fire sucking air...

The woman is cotton-haired, but not quite frail,
and the black hand digging
                              into the pocket of her coat
brings out a coin purse, red and blue beaded,
like something you might buy
on a reservation.

Wood crackles
as the door cries low on cold hinges...

Cheated again, they see,
                              and a glassy angularity hardens
on those faces
as though each has seen history for what it is
and not for what he's imagined.

We go on now
building on what they were obliged to build on,
pasting into the memory
                    these little scraps of consequence
and self-acquittal,

so that it's Amen finally to what can't be changed,
to the noise of headline and newscast, feint
and bluff of history,
while the real thing
                    plays out quietly somewhere else...

like my grandfather rocking up
out of his chair,
                    not gauging their faces,
not glancing at me watching, stunned, from the feed room
as the woman fingered coins
and lifted from the drink box a bottle of Coca-Cola,
so that suddenly at the scripted moment
the script fell away,
                    his hand simply opening,
his head nodding slowly
as she dropped the two nickels and faded
in the drizzle, in the shiver and groan of muffler,
the crunch of tires on gravel.

And Amen now to that failure of nerve
or heart, or among those hardening glares, that victory
of nerve or heart.

Amen to its passing into memory
and Amen to its passing again out of memory...

Amen even to the Kmart where his grocery stood,
and the five-stall barn sagging toward the riding ring,
the hillside of pasture,
                    the kudzued chicken houses
and dog lots,
            the baseball field of my father's making
with its twelve-foot wire backstop...

Amen to the leaving behind of places
that might have been less lovely and often are...

and to the dust that walked those places
to enter by its own path
                    this fractured afterlife of memory,
and peace to the souls that abandoned that dust,
                                        Amen.

Each evening the light forgives the darkness,
each morning the darkness forgives
the light,
            and after the final flame has fallen off
the tongue, the silence that forgives everything...
the loosed soul tumbling...

And Amen also to single-malt Scotch in the emerald dusk,
and this child with the rake-handle

taller than her head,
muscling her will against the inevitable...

What's left in these last moments but memory?
And what is memory
but the mirror image of hope?

So Amen also to hope
and to these blurred receding thoughts of the evening
blowing out across the lawn furniture
                                    and barbecue grill,
leaf-drifts and scattering wind,
                          these shadows
of house and pine

and fence and maple becoming one shadow
when the shadows of this life...
                          yes,
lengthen into the shadow of memory,

and finally
to that shadow, Amen.

PART IV

A Walk to Carter's Lake

Look, above the creek, hummingbirds in the trumpet vine.
Not too close, wait. See the green blurs
stitching the leaves?

Here at the edge of the millennium
I don't imagine
you'd call them anything as archaic as angels.

But aren't they agents of a sort, and secret,
dissolving and solidifying,
spying from their constantly shifting perches of air,
always nervous
of us, risking only a stab
in a bell of petals?

Don't look so stunned, lay your pack
in the needles and catch a breath. I know,
you thought you knew me,
and now to hear me talk this way...

I'm glad I've stopped pretending
to love people
and the cities where people can't love themselves.
This is what the quiet accomplishes,
and the water trusting
the shadows to eventually peel back to the trees.

Small wonder the angels are said to despise us.
Still, without them
how do we account for our meanness?

Look at that, what else can promenade
in the air? And how easily
they're alarmed,
revving off into the mist.

A Canoe

remembering James Dickey

Racket below us,
diesel clank
and the grate of linked steel, and on that hillside of graves
we laid down our charcoal and rice paper
to watch at yard speed and rising
a rolling curtain of freight cars blocking out the river.
Tombstones trembled near trackside – coal car,
boxcar, tanker, transport –
then behind the last wheel rattling around the crypts,
far up toward the highway, near the middle of the river,
a canoe washed under the bridge.
Red canoe. Empty.

Screech of the freight disappearing,
then a lazy ride, the canoe,
                                        so we let our eyes go
with it. River untroubled, calm reflection.

On the far bank, shadowy,
three fishermen on the rocks pushed back their hats.
Long canes wagging in a glint of sunlight,
lines swept down
                        toward the hunger of carp...
they only slouched lower in their lawn chairs.

What deeper stirring could they hope for?
A metaphor untethered, loose
and retrievable,
                but drifting away...

Night Company

In her robe the young widow boils chocolate.

The house is dark, only a candle stub
gasping on the table,
and through the narrow window she watches moonlight
edging over the pines.
Last night she drank hot cider, fresh, a gift,
but tonight she feels like something rich, the cobbler
wrapped in foil in the fridge,
or one of her husband's little cigars.

Hunger isn't something she's easy with yet,
but she feels a slight lift
as she stirs the chocolate into the boiling milk.

Over the fields the howl
of dogs, and she cuts the eye of the stove.

She's glad her neighbors have stopped visiting,
are baking their cakes and pies
for the sick. Apricot dressing, turkey,
okra, two days old, and the lid ajar on the garbage.

Soon she'll blow out the candle, sit by the window
and nurse her cup. The moon will climb
as the stars drip steadily into the woods.

And if she's quiet,
if enough shadow falls across the house, her sister
may come again down the ridge, rustling leaves,
wary as a lover, to skulk
under the apple tree and clothesline, dragging
out of the shadows, one by one,
her three bushy cubs.

Heron Blues

Across the night clouds a wash of purple light,
a sheen on the pavement
and the brick storefronts turning pink – Frontier Drugs,
Zoo City Herbs, the painted windows
of the Stockman's Bar.
The whole town looks asleep.

But say a stranger, parting the hotel's dusty curtains, catches
odd wings in the streetlamp.
What would he think of the great blue heron
throwing it's shadow over Main,
over the gables of City Hall, the fountain
and gazebo, the town's one traffic light
tinting the empty streets?
Maybe he turns to shake his wife, then thinks again,
knowing this luck is momentary.

Once in Florida I climbed down a metal stairway
into a cavern lit by water.
Behind green glass the big fish lulled
in muted color. It was something
like being asleep though I knew I wasn't –
the lazy sea bass, the tigers, the circling jacks
and grouper. Then out of the rocks
a black wing flapped the window –
when I caught myself it was gone, a swirl
of sand off the bottom.

Later in sleep it frightened me again, and I woke
into blue shadows, stunned
and curious, and went to the window.
A spread of giant wings dragged a shadow over
the rooftops. For a long time after
I stared at the clouds
and puzzled the talent the world shows for mystery,
sending these glimpses on wings.

Living Lingerie: In the Modeling Parlor

The sign itself is a shab you need, blue neon half-circling
a curvy silhouette. And rain spilling the gutters
seems the perfect stage effect.
Any minute the building could crumble
like your favorite fantasy.

But the dreadlocked woman, who touches you only
with her eyes, waits on the sofa
in the picture window,
crossing her legs on faded floral, a postcard
in the neon tinting the glass.

Down the hall to a room she guides you.
A tape in the boom box, and the bass of reggae
weaves around her hips. A lamp
dulls a wall mirror and her blush flares.
She looks younger than you remember,
and, distracted, you imagine
what she might go home to –
                              a boyfriend asleep
on the sofa? or the snore of a window fan,
cold dinner in the fridge? About being alone
she may know as much as you.

Only for a moment are you ashamed
of not asking – that comes later, with single-malt

nightcaps. She turns in the mirror
to unbutton her dress,
her company now an ideal loneliness.

Steve Belew Plays the National Steel

Red sparks
of the mosquito-coil sizzling on an orange crate,
my own drunk face, move in the face
of his chrome guitar.
The bottleneck grazes strings,
and watchdogs grow quiet in the Holiness churchyard.
On the corner of Gress, a prison widow rocks
on her porch, pours sloe gin
from bottle to cup. An aquarium lamps
her doorway, her Chihuahua sleeps in a flowerpot.
Guitar notes float over hedges
and walls, families of draped laundry
ghosting the projects,
and under the leaves of mimosa and oak,
her children have opened their windows –
fighting sleep, they curl,
listening with their eyes closed.

For beauty we sometimes have to close our eyes –
as I do now, rocked
against the railing of this deck,
hearing in these sparks of glass and steel
a woman dragging the Dumpsters
of the Claremont Hotel.
Down alleys off Ponce, in a peacoat
and cap, she parades under smutty windows,

not drunk, I think, but slightly dazed
by her own vagrant grace, limping
in jogging shoes
on the steaming asphalt, pushing
in a junked-up grocery cart
her battered Truetone archtop.

All over the yard, the bottleneck loosens
the tongues of trees. They sway
like drunks to a jukebox.
I sway and, through the coil's red burn,
gaze over that cart
into a shelter of trembling cardboard.
There the alley narrows
into dimness, windows curtained
in the dull apartments, sky
smudged between roofs.
Who knows what promise floats over these shadows
or whether it rings as true
in that refuge of boxes,
though I hear her fingers fumbling the neck,
fretting for a key,
until somewhere above the long alley
a window opens.

A Room on Washington Avenue

On your way to meet a client
at Mick's or that other restaurant in Underground
your secretary sends you to, the one with the French name
you always mispronounce, you detour again through the park.
A month of heat and even the pigeons look oppressed,
slack and dopey in the green shade
of the cherry trees. But here you are, two blocks
out of your way and sweating in the thick light going
watery green, craning around the fountain
to catch the bench where a girl in headphones
sits with her legs crossed, smoking.
Her hair is shorter today and black as your shoe.

All right, you say, *a girl.* Because that's what she is,
fourteen, fifteen, and you mean it
as a chide for gawking.
But no good. Even the way she holds her cigarette
is like the hand slowly vanishing in the room
you carry with you.

You admire again her fingers turning a page,
that slender wrist hovering over the chipped-iron footboard,
as vague now as those mystic guitars
distorting through the hi-fi. That streetlamp
behind the blue magnolia, the filmy curtain,
tobacco smoke, incense –

there's always uncertain light in a memory like this,
and you could stumble through that haze for years
without finding your way to the door.

At the Grave of Martha Ellis

Today a visitor has left a rose
at your feet
and a few of the yellow buds sprouting on the hillside,
a quarter to buy whatever it will in your stilled childhood
of 1896. Misty rain
and no sun for days, the silky tongues
of the cherry blossoms struggle at their morning prayers,
the willow and the winged elm, the mulberry
and the sweet gum
spread their budding gospel down Hawthorne Ridge.
Little Martha, these mornings of early mist
when the sun hasn't quite cleared
the carriage paths
and the breeze up the hillside oozes
honeysuckle and cherry,
the soul likes to cruise for serenity.

But you know why I've come.
Before the stone carvers turned you into marble,
you knew what it was to wander among angels,
gathering from these terraces
your Sunday bouquets while waltzers around the bandstand
strayed into the graves. Little Martha,
in middle age rebirth isn't such easy work,
though everything goes at it again
like Baptists reeling to articulate rapture,

and the morning reissues its pledge –
the mockingbird,
the crow breaking the far hush of the wind,
and in the valley above the river
white clouds of dogwood floating through the underbrush
while redwings drop like blood
through the branches.

A Morning from the Gospel of John

for Reynolds Price

This morning in my bathroom mirror, I glimpsed the slope
of my shoulders, my chest thinning to a hint of ribs,
the hair of my pouching belly
black and beaded with water,
and pondering myself limp and priestly,
laced with blue veins, I judged nothing threatening.
Sometimes, I admit, I even look at this unremarkable body
which is beautiful only
in design, and feel a laughable joy.

So of what is the body to be mindful?

And I remembered the disciples who fished all night
on the sea of Tiberias
only to come in at daybreak, their boat empty.
From the shore a stranger asks what they've caught.
Nothing. Then throw to the starboard.
And there they net more fish
than they can haul. I like to think of Simon Peter
when he first catches that voice, how in one translation
he tucks up, not girds on, his shirt.
I study that moment he jumps from the boat, eyes
on the shore, hands
lifting shirt over legs, groin, hips.
I love to imagine being startled
into innocence, heedless
of the body leaping naked toward God.

In the Wilderness

Over burnt fields, drift of crows and chimney smoke,
the gruel of twilight lowers the sky.
One wagon on the road, a horse in the traces,
no rider. The gate hangs open
on the meetinghouse fence,
wind points the vane toward the river.

All day he's labored in this mood, lost
and ill, remembering
the water over the scrubbing stone, the canopy
of oaks where two Sabbaths last
a mother, accused, knelt in the roots
to touch the face
of her strangled child. Newborn.
He pictures the mouth drooling mud,
gray eyes the gloss
of oyster shells, fine hair
tangled like straw. And hovering
over the cheek, the mother's finger
trembling, a faint blush
bearing witness under her fingertip.
Three days on a gibbet above the river
her body hosted birds.

He touches a finger to the leaded glass –
a certain frost, and the night

could bring snow –
then glances at his book lying
open on the table, the smoky tallow sputtering
in the draft. His eyes are weak,
the season's dimmed the house.
A ship's bell, and the Reverend snuffs
the wick. An evening walk
would be restful, to the river and the docks,
but tomorrow requires
a sermon, the temptation
in the wilderness. And the wind is up,
the west wind, out of the wilderness,
and true to the season
the whole sky is overcast with God.

PART V

My Uncle Sowing Beatitudes

1

When he huffed out of the woods at the foot of the hill,
both fists clenched rocks. My uncle saw him
before he reached the field,
and stopped hoeing,
stood up and leaned on his hoe.
This was a cousin on his father's side,
nineteen or twenty, and a week out of jail.

Far off in the okra a wind whirled the dust,
a rustle of needles
sparked the tree line. He screamed something
I don't recall, he kicked the dirt,
he wanted to fight. He was drunk
and sick of his mother nagging
about the muddy well.
My uncle's tractor had been causing a runoff.

Or it hadn't, my uncle said,
the well was almost half a mile away.
But the boy threw hard out of the sunlight
and caught him on the cheek,
and my uncle wobbled,
a little dazed.

2

I pop the clip
from the pistol and cross that same field fertile
now only in memory. The woods are quieted
from the shots, and the field is quiet,
in the far distance stretching toward the road
only one indignant crow.

Four bullets clustered in the heart of the target,
three more in wounding range –
good enough.

Listen, here in the foothills
above the suburban skirmishes of apparent Armageddon,
I can't turn around without having
to untangle parable.
I run a fist into a coat pocket, loose change
of cartridges. All over the ground,
sunlight on spent brass.

3

Bastard, coward,
I remember those names, and the boy spitting
and pointing his finger.   .
Dust rose again behind them
and the small sky darkened with vultures.

Vultures?
          No, but in middle age the memory circles.

So my uncle only turns again to his hoe,
his chopped strokes and drags,
edgy hacking at clods,
and he isn't a small man, early forties,
stout, an ex-marine who'd out-toughed the Japanese
on Guadalcanal. (Could thirty years
completely cloud his shadow?)
He hoes his beans until the boy disappears,
then brushes the cut with the back
of his wrist.
        I recall this about him,
along with the morning
he crouched for hours beside an icy creek
only to balk at shooting a buck.
In Paradise, he may have said,
not even the violence of a heartbeat.

A Sunday Dinner

I

Mosquito and tick
on that island of mud, centipede, fly, scorpion, lice,
all breed of bug, as she told it,
but mostly mosquitoes – yellow clouds smoking off
the mangrove swamps – and so with exhaustion and hunger
the long hazy weakness of malaria.
Or if you were lucky
you only starved, dug in with your pound of captured rice
for the green flares on parachutes
and banzai screams charging from the jungle.
Water was there
at your feet, in whatever hole was handy.

He wasn't so lucky, my uncle.
When he could sleep
he snatched it on his back in a floorless tent,
oozed down in mud and the waves of chill and convulsive
      fever,
for hours grenades going off
in his brain and hot colors swimming,
sizzle and shell thud, and the jungle growing tongues –
obscenity in broken English, suck
of boots in mud
or the horrible suck and wheeze of the wounded,

and sometimes up from the beach
those silky horns and clarinets –
Dorsey, Miller,
Goodman – the sad honey voice
of Tokyo Rose...

2

They wouldn't talk, she said, pointing with her knife.
Not my uncle, not my father
lost on those waters for fifteen months
and his family on their prayer-bones nightly
at the altar of Oakdale Baptist.
                                        And that dread
of memory? A fear of eternity,
that onslaught of past into future?

No rice on the table for years...
green beans, peppers, yellow corn, okra, not much
that didn't come from his garden.
No, they wouldn't talk, though once in early marriage
on a corner of their bed,
he held her hand for almost an hour
in a story of men on their knees in the mud,
mouths open for the wafer,
and tried to describe the sweetness on his tongue
when he understood finally
no troops were coming.

3

So until the end
this is as close as we can come to 1942, to Guadalcanal
and that Friday the thirteenth of stars and no moon,
the fragrance of tropical flowers and sweet gases
of decaying flesh,
as clearly as we can see the searchlight
he caught from his hill as it stabbed across the sound
to target the bridge of the cruiser *Atlanta,*
where my father and his gun crew
were already spinning turret number six
as the first shells blasted out that light
and the ocean caught fire
with flares and the big guns spitting,

and as close as we can hold him, who watched
through fever with his unsaid thoughts,
which we can't know
until the end, and lived to see
fresh troops hit the beach,
so that years later he could meet my father,
who had floated all night near death
in that water, and never mention the war,
though he would marry the man's sister
and scratch out a living on used cars and cattle
and ponder his happiness,
and share with her once his first glimpse of peace
when tumbling through a night between drifts of sleep,
over crackle of tide and insect, groan

and scrap of prayer, a moment neared stillness
as a cockatoo screeched
between sniper fire.

Occurrence in the Big Sky

I

Logs uncaulked, walls all stud
and rough board, plumbing dangling like loose bones,
vents gaping in the hallway
and switch boxes
spilling wires, the furnace still crated on blocks
in the yard of knapweed and dust...
The faucet ticks onto a greasy plate
and wind rakes a tarp
off the porch.

An old woman with a weak heart,
at the kitchen table, near nightfall, ponders
the congested emptiness, at a loss
among hammer and power saw, chisel blade and level,
drills with their blued bits scattered among shavings,
deadbolts and the knobs of doors,
an overturned thermos,
a red handkerchief draped on a sawhorse.
The moon chills her window,
the women from church are late with her supper.
She stares across the room at an unlaced boot,
a gray wool sock worn thin
at the heel –
        Just tell me the time,
don't build me a clock –

and dreads the cleaning out of closets,
the smell of old shirts.

2

And how hard for the soul
to put down the hammer, to understand the last nail
is never driven
and square itself to the blueprint,
to brush off desire
and responsibility like a day's worth of sawdust
and walk through an untrimmed doorway
into a windy field, nothing
on the horizon but the signal fires of angels.

How dizzy the soul must be
floating in that first violent gust of timelessness,
that flurry of images we can hardly imagine,
tumble of face over landscape,
gust of past and future dovetailing.
How it must miss in early evening
something as solid as a bar of chocolate
or a hand across a table.

Rocks grate down the cliffside,
the tin roof
rattles on the guinea coop. Still the soul
must grow happy singing under the hill
in that network of roots,
or pitching its voice
to the needles and wind.

3

In the Cabinet Mountains
of western Montana
I saw something in the sky like a page from Revelation –
high against a white ridge of clouds, two eagles
fighting over a kill. You couldn't tell
from that distance
what they were pulling between them, something large
and black
balled in their talons –

then they dropped it

and falling it uncoiled, twisted and flipped,
a live rope in midair
tumbling itself into loops, into bows,
then straightened
and curled
as though trying to bite its tail –

a few seconds of horror, or ecstasy,
or beauty,
before an eagle plunged
and caught it, rose and broke the clouds.

Notes

"Bronchitis": Kennesaw Mountain is located in Cobb County, Georgia, about twenty miles northwest of Atlanta. On June 27, 1864, it was the site of a crucial engagement in Sherman's Atlanta Campaign. Estimated casualties: Union, 3,000; Confederate, 1,000.

"On Methodist Hill": The former First Methodist Church of Canton, Georgia, and Riverview Cemetery, which rests behind it, sit on a hill overlooking the Etowah River. The building in this poem, the third on this site, was dedicated in 1926 and abandoned by its congregation in 1992 for a larger building outside of town.

"The Widower": Lee Noah Bottoms. September 21, 1894–March 6, 1983.

"The Fisherman and the Little Fish": Aesop.

"Country Store and Moment of Grace": The L.N. Bottoms Store was a two-room general store located on Highway 5, two miles south of Canton, Georgia. It was demolished in the mid-1980s, along with his house, barn, riding ring, chicken houses, and dog lots. The six-acre site is now a Kmart shopping center. The Ralph Bunche School was the local black high school, named after the U.S. diplomat and winner of the 1950 Nobel Prize for Peace. The mill is the Canton Cotton Mill, founded in 1899 and vital to the community for almost eighty years. The USS *Atlanta,* on which my father served, was sunk in the naval battle of Guadalcanal, November 13, 1942. The lines "when the shadows / of this life have grown" are from "I'll Fly Away," words and music by gospel songwriter Albert Brumley.

"A Canoe": Rose Hill Cemetery, Macon, Georgia.

"Heron Blues": A poster by the Montana artist Monte Dolack.

"At the Grave of Martha Ellis": Rose Hill Cemetery, Macon, Georgia. A statue of the twelve-year-old child stands at the head of her grave. The inscription on her stone reads: "Our Baby. She was love personified and her memory is a sweet solace by day, and pleasant dreams by night to Momma, Papa, brothers, and sisters. We will meet again in the sweet bye and bye." Much attention has been drawn to the grave by the song "Little Martha," written by Duane Allman. People in Macon occasionally leave coins and flowers on her stone.

"A Morning from the Gospel of John": This poem grew out of Reynolds Price's fascinating translation of The Good News According to John, found in his *Three Gospels*.

"Occurrence in the Big Sky": Paradise and Wild Horse Plains, Montana.

About the Author

David Bottoms was born in Canton, Georgia, in 1949. He is the author of four other books of poetry and two novels. Among his many awards are the Walt Whitman Award of the Academy of American Poets, the Levinson Prize, an Ingram Merrill Award, an Award in Literature from the American Academy and Institute of Arts and Letters, and fellowships from the National Endowment for the Arts and the John Simon Guggenheim Foundation. He lives with his wife and daughter in Atlanta, where he teaches at Georgia State University.

The Chinese character for poetry (*shih*) combines "word" and "temple." It also serves as raison d'être for Copper Canyon Press.

Founded in 1972, Copper Canyon publishes extraordinary work – from Nobel laureates to emerging poets – and strives to maintain the highest standards of design, manufacture, marketing, and distribution. Our commitment is nurtured and sustained by the community of readers, writers, booksellers, librarians, teachers, students – everyone who shares the conviction that poetry clarifies and deepens social and spiritual awareness.

Great books depend on great presses. Publication of great poetry is especially dependent on the informed appreciation and generous patronage of readers. By becoming a Friend of Copper Canyon Press you can secure the future – and the legacy – of one of the finest independent publishers in America.

For information and catalogs:

COPPER CANYON PRESS
Post Office Box 271
Port Townsend, Washington 98368
360/385-4925
coppercanyon@olympus.net
www.ccpress.org

This book set in
Sabon, designed by
Jan Tschichold.
Book interior design
by Valerie Brewster.
Printed on archival-
quality Glatfelter
Author's Text
by McNaughton
& Gunn.